C

My
Two Dads

Julie Murray

Abdo Kids Junior
is an Imprint of Abdo Kids
abdobooks.com

Abdo

THIS IS MY FAMILY

Kids

abdobooks.com

Published by Abdo Kids, a division of ABDO, P.O. Box 398166, Minneapolis, Minnesota 55439.
Copyright © 2021 by Abdo Consulting Group, Inc. International copyrights reserved in all countries.
No part of this book may be reproduced in any form without written permission from the publisher.
Abdo Kids Junior™ is a trademark and logo of Abdo Kids.

Printed in the United States of America, North Mankato, Minnesota.

052020

092020

 THIS BOOK CONTAINS
RECYCLED MATERIALS

Photo Credits: iStock, Media Bakery, Shutterstock

Production Contributors: Teddy Borth, Jennie Forsberg, Grace Hansen

Design Contributors: Candice Keimig, Pakou Moua, Dorothy Toth

Library of Congress Control Number: 2019955590

Publisher's Cataloging-in-Publication Data

Names: Murray, Julie, author.

Title: My two dads / by Julie Murray

Description: Minneapolis, Minnesota : Abdo Kids, 2021 | Series: This is my family | Includes online
    resources and index.

Identifiers: ISBN 9781098202248 (lib. bdg.) | ISBN 9781644943922 (pbk.) | ISBN 9781098203221 (ebook)
    | ISBN 9781098203719 (Read-to-Me ebook)

Subjects: LCSH: Families--Juvenile literature. | Same-sex parents--Juvenile literature. | Children of same-
    sex parents--Juvenile literature. | Parent and child--Juvenile literature. | Families--Social aspects—
    Juvenile literature.

Classification: DDC 306.85--dc23

Table of Contents

My Two Dads

Jacob has two dads. They like to walk the dog together.

Maria reads with her dads.

They like funny books.

9

Jay is at the park. He plays soccer with his dads.

Tyler **preps** dinner with his dads. They are having salad.